Mighty Machines

Fighter Planes

by Matt Doeden

Consulting Editor: Gail Saunders-Smith, PhD

Capstone
press

Mankato, Minnesota

Pebble Plus is published by Capstone Press,
151 Good Counsel Drive, P.O. Box 669, Mankato, Minnesota 56002.
www.capstonepress.com

1 2 3 4 5 6 10 09 08 07 06 05

Library of Congress Cataloging-in-Publication Data
Doeden, Matt.
    Fighter planes / by Matt Doeden.
    p. cm.—(Pebble plus: mighty machines)
    Includes bibliographical references and index.
    ISBN 0-7368-3657-8 (hardcover)
    ISBN 0-7368-5138-0 (paperback)
    1. Fighter planes—Juvenile literature. I. Title. II. Series.
UG1242.F5D563 2005
623.74'64—dc22   2004012655

Summary: Simple text and photographs present fighter planes, their parts, and their crew.

Editorial Credits
Martha E. H. Rustad, editor; Molly Nei , set designer; Kate Opseth and Ted Williams, book designers;
    Jo Miller, photo researcher; Scott Thoms, photo editor

Photo Credits
Corbis/George Hall, cover, 10–11, 16–17, 18–19
Corel, 1
DVIC/Master Sgt Lochner, 21
Ted Carlson/Fotodynamics, 4–5, 6–7, 8–9, 12–13, 14–15

Note to Parents and Teachers

The Mighty Machines set supports national standards related to science, technology, and society. This book describes and illustrates fighter planes. The images support early readers in understanding the text. The repetition of words and phrases helps early readers learn new words. This book also introduces early readers to subject-specific vocabulary words, which are defined in the Glossary section. Early readers may need assistance to read some words and to use the Table of Contents, Glossary, Read More, Internet Sites, and Index sections of the book.

Table of Contents

What Are Fighter Planes?

Fighter planes are
very fast planes.
Militaries use
fighter planes in battles.

Fighter planes often
fly together.
They fly in lines.

Parts of Fighter Planes

Fighter planes have
long, wide wings.
Wings help planes
fly and turn.

Jet engines push fighter

planes through the air.

The engines are

inside the planes.

Fighter planes carry missiles
and guns for fighting.
The guns are inside the planes.
Some planes carry bombs.

bomb

missile

Landing gear helps
fighter planes take off
and land. Wing flaps help
planes move up and down.

wing flap

landing gear

15

Pilots

Pilots fly fighter planes.

They sit in the cockpit.

TSG W AKIONA

Pilots wear masks and flight suits. This gear keeps them safe during flights.

19

Mighty Machines

Pilots fly fighter planes
in battles. Fighter planes
are mighty machines.

21

Glossary

battle—a fight between two military groups

cockpit—the place where a pilot sits in a plane

flight suit—a one-piece suit that protects a pilot

gear—equipment or clothing

jet engine—an engine that uses streams of hot gas to make power

landing gear—a set of wheels under an airplane; the wheels are down when the plane takes off and lands; the wheels stay hidden inside the plane when it is in the air.

mask—a face covering worn by a pilot; the mask gives oxygen for breathing.

military—the armed forces of a country

missile—a weapon that flies and blows up when it hits a target; pilots aim missiles at targets such as enemy planes.

pilot—a person who flies aircraft

Read More

Baysura, Kelly. *Military Planes.* Flying Machines. Vero Beach, Fla.: Rourke, 2001.

Bingham, Caroline. *DK Big Book of Airplanes.* Airplanes. New York: Dorling Kindersley, 2001.

Doeden, Matt. *The U.S. Air Force.* The U.S. Armed Forces. Mankato, Minn.: Blazers, 2005.

Internet Sites

FactHound offers a safe, fun way to find Internet sites related to this book. All of the sites on FactHound have been researched by our staff.

Here's how:

1. Visit *www.facthound.com*

2. Type in this special code **0736836578** for age-appropriate sites. Or enter a search word related to this book for a more general search.

3. Click on the **Fetch It** button.

FactHound will fetch the best sites for you!

Index

Word Count: 115
Grade: 1
Early-Intervention Level: 15